Henry David's House

Henry David Thoreau

Edited by Steven Schnur

Illustrated by Peter Fiore

Charlesbridge

For Ron and Mike, builders of dreams
—S. S.

For my mother, Rose
—P. F.

All the words in this book are Thoreau's own, taken from the first edition of
Walden, or Life in the Woods, published in August 1854 by Ticknor and Fields.

2007 First paperback edition
Compilation copyright © 2002 by Steven Schnur
Illustrations copyright © 2002 by Peter Fiore
All rights reserved, including the right of reproduction in whole or in part in any form.
Charlesbridge and colophon are registered trademarks of Charlesbridge Publishing, Inc.

Published by Charlesbridge
85 Main Street, Watertown, MA 02472
(617) 926-0329
www.charlesbridge.com

Library of Congress Cataloging-in-Publication Data
Thoreau, Henry David, 1817-1862.
  [Walden, Selections]
  Henry David's House / Henry David Thoreau ; edited by Steven Schnur.
    p. cm.
  Summary: Excerpts from Thoreau's *Walden* highlight his belief in the inherent value of living
life in harmony with nature.
  ISBN 978-0-88106-116-1 (reinforced for library use)
  ISBN 978-0-88106-117-8 (softcover)
  1. Thoreau, Henry David, 1817–1862—Homes and haunts—Massachusetts—Walden Pond Region
(Middlesex County)—Juvenile literature. 2. Walden Pond Region (Middlesex County, Mass.)—
Biography—Juvenile literature. 3. Authors, American—19th century—Biography—Juvenile literature.
[1. Thoreau, Henry David, 1817–1862. 2. Authors, American.] I. Schnur, Steven. II. Title.
  PS3048.A3 2002
  818'.303—dc21
                                                                    2001002620

Printed in China
(hc) 10 9 8 7 6 5 4 3 2
(sc) 10 9 8 7 6 5 4 3 2 1

Illustrations done in watercolor and oil on Strathmore illustration board
Display type and text type set in Galliard
Color separations by Bright Arts Graphics, Singapore
Printed and bound by Regent Publishing Services, China
Production supervision by Brian G. Walker
Designed by Diane M. Earley

Every spirit builds itself a house,
and beyond its house a world,
and beyond its world a heaven.
—*Ralph Waldo Emerson*

Near the end of March I borrowed an axe
and went down to the woods by Walden Pond
and began to cut down some tall white pines
for timber.

It was a pleasant hillside where I worked, covered
with pine woods, through which I looked out
on the pond. The ice in the pond was not yet
dissolved, though there were some open spaces,
and it was all dark colored and saturated
with water.

On the 1st of April it rained and melted the ice, and in the early part of the day, which was very foggy, I heard a stray goose groping about over the pond and cackling as if lost, or like the spirit of the fog.

So I went on for some days cutting and hewing timber, and also studs and rafters, all with my narrow axe, singing to myself.

My days in the woods were not very long ones; yet I usually carried my dinner of bread and butter, and read the newspaper in which it was wrapped, at noon, sitting amid the green pine boughs which I had cut off. Sometimes a rambler in the wood was attracted by the sound of my axe, and we chatted pleasantly over the chips which I had made.

By the middle of April my house was framed and ready for the raising. I had already bought the shanty of James Collins, an Irishman who worked on the Fitchburg Railroad, for boards.

I took down this dwelling, drawing the nails, and removed it to the pond side by small cart-loads. One early thrush gave me a note or two as I drove along the woodland path.

I dug my cellar in the side of a hill sloping to the south, where a woodchuck had formerly dug his burrow, down through sumach and blackberry roots, six feet square by seven deep, to a fine sand where potatoes would not freeze in any winter.

At length, in the beginning of May, with the help of some of my acquaintances, I set up the frame of my house.

I began to occupy my house on the 4th of July, as soon as it was boarded and roofed, but before boarding I laid the foundation of a chimney at one end, bringing two cartloads of stones up the hill from the pond in my arms.

I built the chimney after my hoeing in the fall, before a fire became necessary for warmth, doing my cooking in the mean while out of doors on the ground, early in the morning.

I have thus a tight shingled and plastered house, ten feet wide by fifteen long, and eight-feet posts, with a garret and a closet, a large window on each side, two trap doors, one door at the end, and a brick fireplace opposite. I have also a small wood-shed adjoining, made chiefly of the stuff which was left after building the house.

My furniture, part of which I made myself, consisted of a bed, a table, a desk, three chairs (one for solitude, two for friendship, three for society), a looking-glass three inches in diameter, a pair of tongs and andirons, a kettle, a skillet, and a frying-pan, a dipper, a wash-bowl, two knives and forks, three plates, one cup, one spoon, a jug for oil, a jug for molasses, and a japanned lamp.

My dwelling was small, but it seemed larger for being a single apartment and remote from neighbors. All the attractions of a house were concentrated in one room; it was kitchen, chamber, parlor, and keeping-room.

Sometimes, in a summer morning, having taken my accustomed bath, I sat in my sunny doorway from sunrise till noon, rapt in a revery, amidst the pines and hickories and sumachs, in undisturbed solitude and stillness, while the birds sang around or flitted noiseless through the house, until by the sun falling in at my west window, or the noise of some traveller's wagon on the distant highway, I was reminded of the lapse of time.

In warm evenings I frequently sat in a boat playing the flute, and saw the perch, which I seemed to have charmed, hovering around me, and the moon travelling over the ribbed bottom, which was strewed with the wrecks of the forest.

By the first of September I saw two or three small maples turned scarlet across the pond. Gradually from week to week the character of each tree came out, and it admired itself reflected in the smooth mirror of the lake.

In October I went a-graping to the river meadows, and loaded myself with clusters more precious for their beauty and fragrance than for food. I collected a small store of wild apples for coddling. When chestnuts were ripe I laid up half a bushel for winter. It was very exciting at that season to roam the boundless chestnut woods with a bag on my shoulder, and a stick to open burrs with in my hand. Occasionally I climbed and shook the trees.

Many a traveller came out of his way to see me and the inside of my house. One real runaway slave, among the rest, whom I helped to forward toward the northstar. Children come a-berrying, railroad men taking a Sunday morning walk in clean shirts, fishermen and hunters, poets and philosophers, in short, all honest pilgrims, who came out to the woods for freedom's sake, and really left the village behind, I was ready to greet.

At length the winter set in in good earnest, just as I had finished plastering, and the wind began to howl around the house.

One night in the beginning of winter, before the pond froze over, I was startled by the loud honking of a goose, and, stepping to the door, heard the sound of their wings like a tempest in the woods as they flew low over my house. A slight sound at evening lifts me up by the ears, and makes life seem inexpressibly grand.

I also heard the whooping of the ice in the pond, as if it were restless in its bed. Sometimes I heard the foxes as they ranged over the snow crust, in moonlight nights, in search of a partridge or other game, barking like forest dogs. Usually the red squirrel waked me in the dawn, coursing over the roof and up and down the sides of the house.

One attraction in coming to the woods to live was that I should have leisure and opportunity to see the Spring come in. In April the pigeons were seen again and in due time I heard the martins twittering over my clearing. Early in May, the oaks, hickories, maples, and other trees, just putting out amidst the pine woods around the pond, imparted a brightness like sunshine to the landscape, especially in cloudy days, as if the sun were breaking through mists and shining faintly on the hillsides here and there.

On the third or fourth of May I saw a loon in the pond, and during the first week of the month I heard the whippoorwill. The phoebe had already come and looked in at my door and window.

We can never have enough of Nature.

Editor's Note

In the spring of 1845 twenty-seven-year-old Henry David Thoreau borrowed an axe from his neighbor, Bronson Alcott, walked two miles from his family's house in Concord, Massachusetts, to the shores of Walden Pond, and began to build himself a house. He had tried to live as others lived—as "a schoolmaster, a private tutor, a surveyor, a gardener, a farmer, a house painter, a carpenter, a mason, a day-laborer, a pencil-maker, a glass-paper maker, a writer," but had found each of those careers disappointing. "The mass of men," he wrote, "lead lives of quiet desperation." He was determined not to be one of them.

So he set off for the woods to build himself a house that would allow the same easy relationship with the wilderness that the American Indians, whom he greatly admired, once enjoyed. There he intended to reflect on nature, society, and the human spirit, to read widely, to keep his journal, and to write. The daily act of setting down in words one's thoughts, observations, and actions elevates and orders those moments, separating them from the great mass of unexamined life. Keeping a daily journal was central to Thoreau's life and art—the very heart of his artistic process. "I went to the woods because I wished to live deliberately," he declared "to front only the essential facts of life, and see if I could not learn what it had to teach, and not, when I came to die, discover that I had not lived." That singular act produced one of the most influential books of nineteenth-century American literature, *Walden, or Life in the Woods*, a volume full of prickly prejudices and invaluable insights that, as another great American writer, E. B. White, observed, "is like an invitation to life's dance."

Thoreau forever changed the way we think about nature and our place in it. Despite Thoreau's lack of recognition during his lifetime, *Walden* became one of the most widely read books of American literature, influencing minds as diverse as Leo Tolstoy, Mahatma Gandhi, and Robert Frost. The unique product of a unique mind, *Walden* is part memoir, part nature study, part do-it-yourself manual, part economic and political treatise, part philosophical tract, part poem, part dream.

Today, Thoreau's cabin lingers in the American consciousness as an image of perfection, the ideal home—modest, spare, uninhibiting, a place in harmony with nature. In our restless search for meaning we return repeatedly to that vision of a man with nothing but an axe walking into the woods and fashioning for himself all that he needs to live honestly and completely: a simple house, Henry David's house.

—*Steven Schnur*

WALDEN POND is in Concord, Massachusetts, about 20 miles outside of Boston. The National Park Service designated Walden Pond as an historic landmark in 1965. In the 1980s, developers had plans to build an office building and condominiums in Walden Woods. Thanks to the efforts of the Walden Woods Project, the endangered lands surrounding the pond were purchased from the developers. Walden Pond State Reservation is open to the public. A replica of Thoreau's house stands there today.